BEGINNING SOLO Guitar

First Fingerstyle Songs

ISBN 978-1-4803-9509-1

HAL•LEONARD® CORPORATION

7777 W. BLUEMOUND RD. P.O. BOX 13819 MILWAUKEE, WI 53213

Visit Hal Leonard Online at
www.halleonard.com

GUITAR NOTATION LEGEND

THE MUSICAL STAFF shows pitches and rhythms and is divided by bar lines into measures. Pitches are named after the first seven letters of the alphabet.

TABLATURE graphically represents the guitar fingerboard. Each horizontal line represents a string, and each number represents a fret.

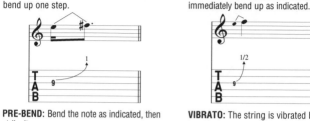

4th string, 2nd fret   1st & 2nd strings open, played together   open D chord

HALF-STEP BEND: Strike the note and bend up 1/2 step.

WHOLE-STEP BEND: Strike the note and bend up one step.

GRACE NOTE BEND: Strike the note and immediately bend up as indicated.

SLIGHT (MICROTONE) BEND: Strike the note and bend up 1/4 step.

BEND AND RELEASE: Strike the note and bend up as indicated, then release back to the original note. Only the first note is struck.

PRE-BEND: Bend the note as indicated, then strike it.

VIBRATO: The string is vibrated by rapidly bending and releasing the note with the fretting hand.

PALM MUTING: The note is partially muted by the pick hand lightly touching the string(s) just before the bridge.

HAMMER-ON: Strike the first (lower) note with one finger, then sound the higher note (on the same string) with another finger by fretting it without picking.

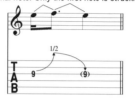

PULL-OFF: Place both fingers on the notes to be sounded. Strike the first note and without picking, pull the finger off to sound the second (lower) note.

LEGATO SLIDE: Strike the first note and then slide the same fret-hand finger up or down to the second note. The second note is not struck.

SHIFT SLIDE: Same as legato slide, except the second note is struck.

TRILL: Very rapidly alternate between the notes indicated by continuously hammering on and pulling off.

TAPPING: Hammer ("tap") the fret indicated with the pick-hand index or middle finger and pull off to the note fretted by the fret hand.

NATURAL HARMONIC: Strike the note while the fret-hand lightly touches the string directly over the fret indicated.

PINCH HARMONIC: The note is fretted normally and a harmonic is produced by adding the edge of the thumb or the tip of the index finger of the pick hand to the normal pick attack.

TREMOLO PICKING: The note is picked as rapidly and continuously as possible.

VIBRATO BAR DIVE AND RETURN: The pitch of the note or chord is dropped a specified number of steps (in rhythm), then returned to the original pitch.

VIBRATO BAR SCOOP: Depress the bar just before striking the note, then quickly release the bar.

VIBRATO BAR DIP: Strike the note and then immediately drop a specified number of steps, then release back to the original pitch.

Additional Musical Definitions

(accent)	•	Accentuate note (play it louder).
(staccato)	•	Play the note short.
D.S. al Coda	•	Go back to the sign (%), then play until the measure marked "*To Coda*," then skip to the section labelled "**Coda**."
D.C. al Fine	•	Go back to the beginning of the song and play until the measure marked "*Fine*" (end).

Fill
• Label used to identify a brief melodic figure which is to be inserted into the arrangement.

N.C.
• Harmony is implied.

• Repeat measures between signs.

1. 2.
• When a repeated section has different endings, play the first ending only the first time and the second ending only the second time.

4 **BLOWIN' IN THE WIND - Bob Dylan**

6 **CAN YOU FEEL THE LOVE TONIGHT - Elton John**

8 **DON'T KNOW WHY - Norah Jones**

10 **EVERY BREATH YOU TAKE - The Police**

14 **THE GODFATHER (LOVE THEME) - Movie Soundtrack**

16 **HALLELUJAH - Jeff Buckley**

19 **HAPPY BIRTHDAY TO YOU - Various**

20 **IN MY LIFE - The Beatles**

22 **LEAN ON ME - Bill Withers**

24 **MOON RIVER - Andy Williams**

26 **NO WOMAN NO CRY - Bob Marley**

30 **OVER THE RAINBOW - Judy Garland**

32 **SCARBOROUGH FAIR/CANTICLE - Simon & Garfunkel**

34 **UNCHAINED MELODY - The Righteous Brothers**

36 **WHAT A WONDERFUL WORLD - Louis Armstrong**

Blowin' in the Wind

Words and Music by Bob Dylan

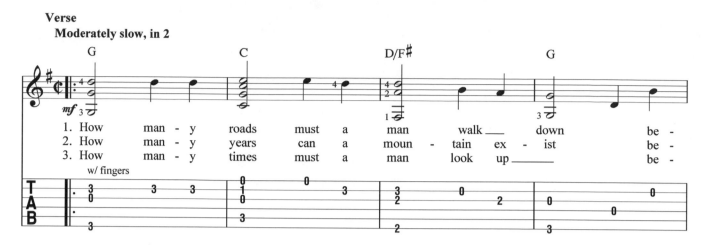

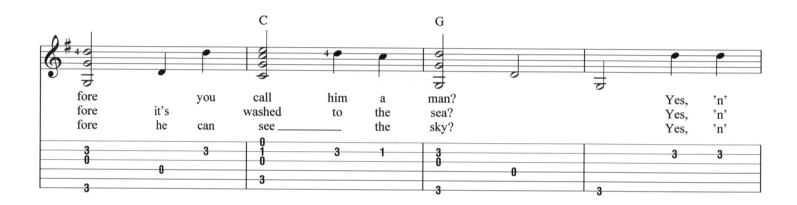

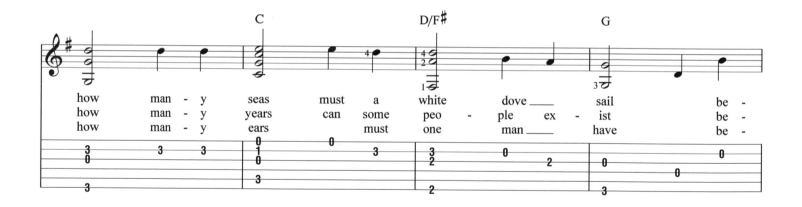

how man - y times must the can - non - balls ___ fly be -
how man - y times can a man turn his head, pre -
how man - y deaths will it take till he knows that

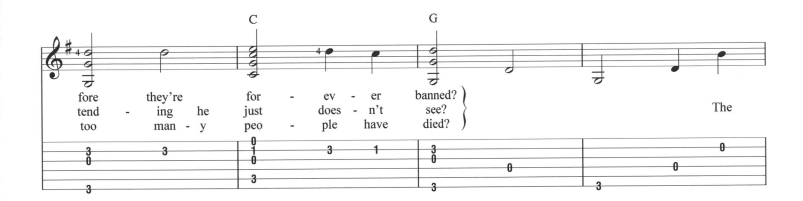

fore they're for - ev - er banned?
tend - ing he just does - n't see?
too man - y peo - ple have died?

The

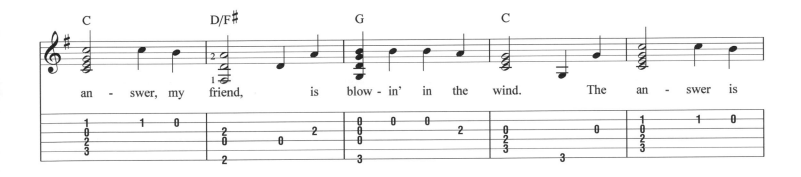

an - swer, my friend, is blow - in' in the wind. The an - swer is

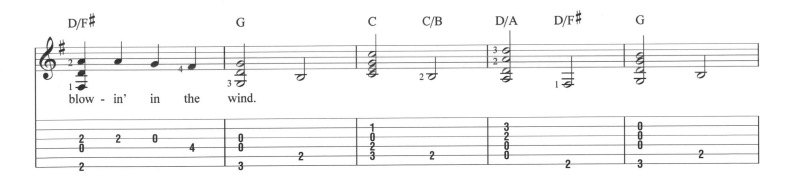

blow - in' in the wind.

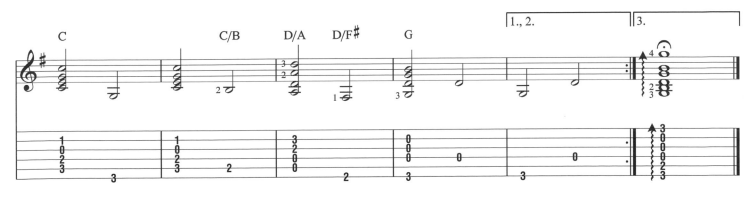

1., 2.   3.

Can You Feel the Love Tonight

from Walt Disney Pictures' THE LION KING

Music by Elton John
Lyrics by Tim Rice

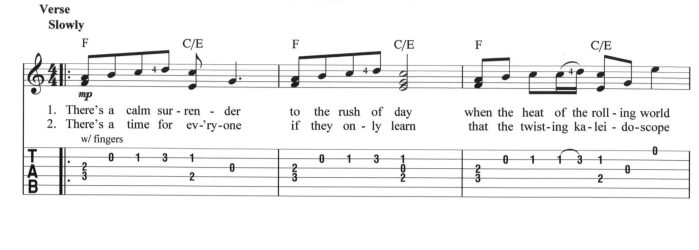

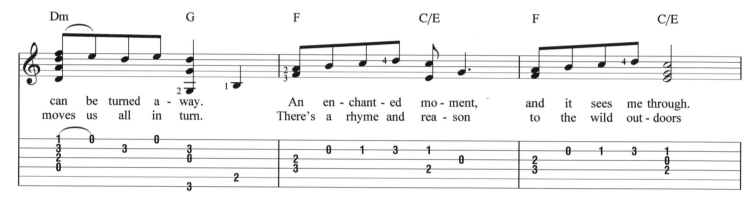

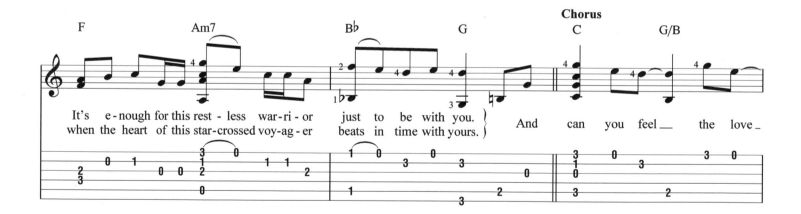

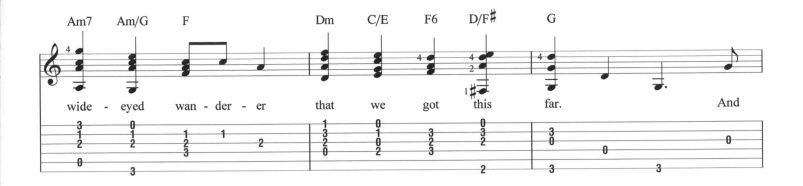

wide - eyed wan - der - er that we got this far. And

can you feel ___ the love ___ to - night, ___ how it's laid to

rest? It's e - nough to make kings and vag - a - bonds be -

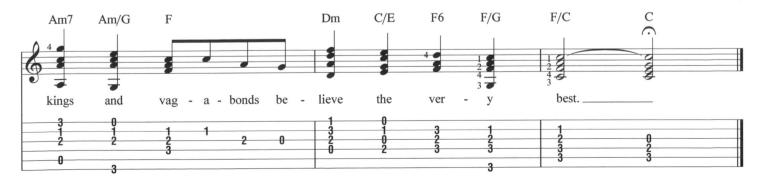

lieve the ver - y best. _____ It's e - nough to make

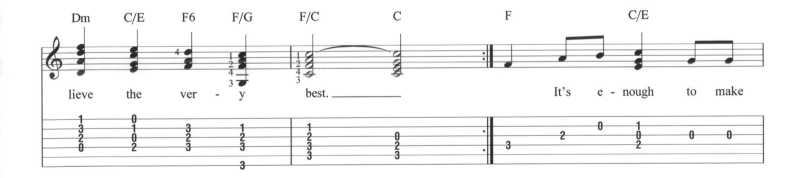

kings and vag - a - bonds be - lieve the ver - y best. _____

Don't Know Why

Words and Music by Jesse Harris

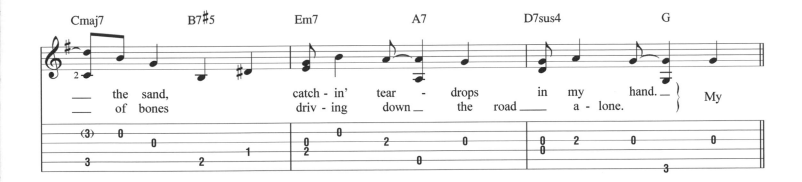

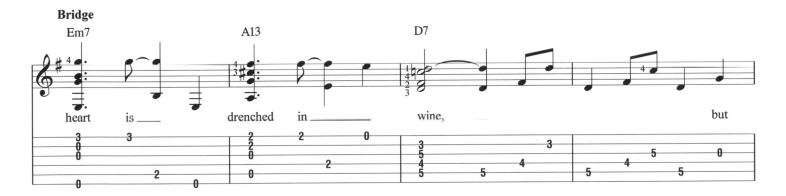

2nd time, D.C. al Coda

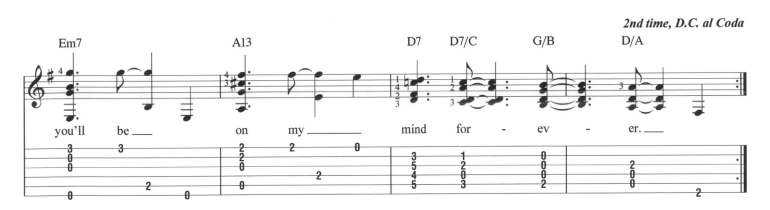

Every Breath You Take

Music and Lyrics by Sting

Intro
Moderately

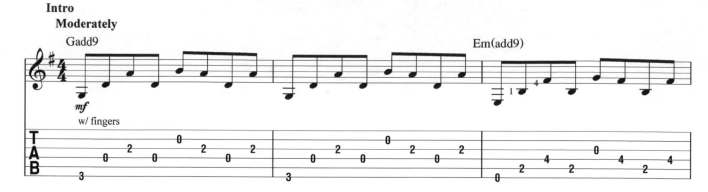

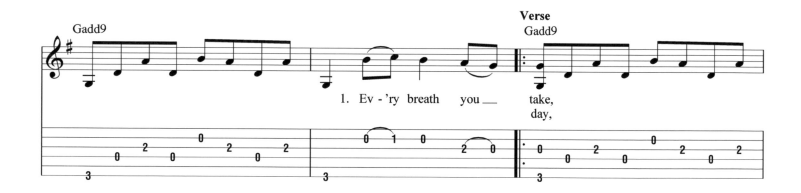

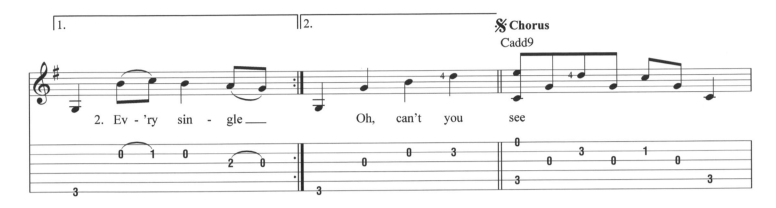

break, ev - 'ry smile___ you fake, ev - 'ry claim you stake,

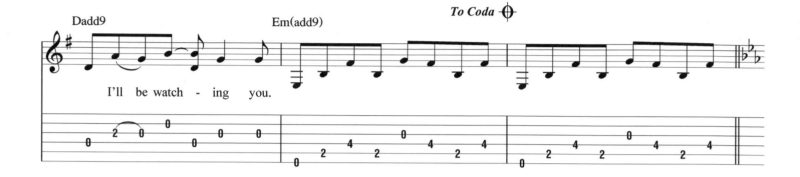

To Coda ⊕

I'll be watch - ing you.

Bridge

Since you've gone___ I been lost with - out___ a trace. I dream at night, I can on -

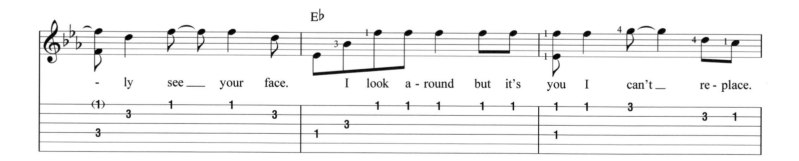

- ly see___ your face. I look a - round but it's you I can't___ re - place.

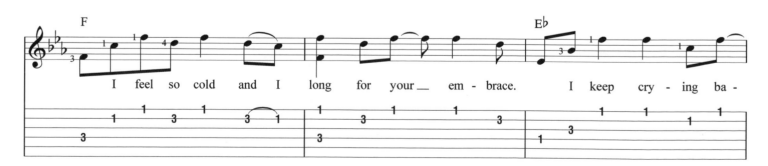

I feel so cold and I long for your___ em - brace. I keep cry - ing ba -

Interlude

- by, ba - by please.

D.S. al Coda

Oh, can't you

Coda

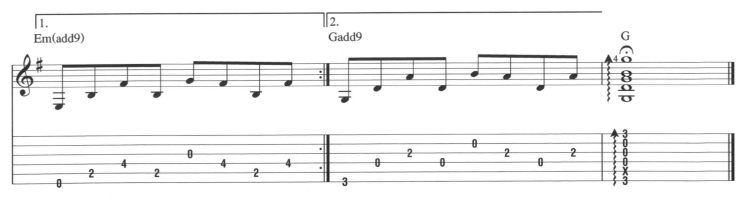

Ev -'ry move — you make, ev -'ry step you take, I'll be watch - ing you.

The Godfather
(Love Theme)
from the Paramount Picture THE GODFATHER
By Nino Rota

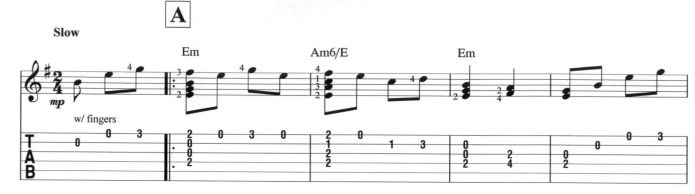

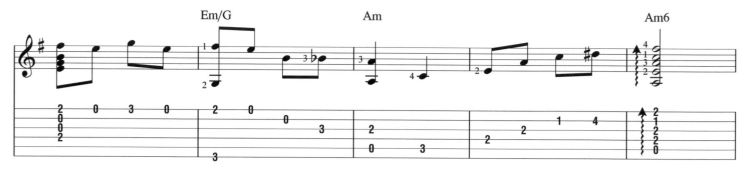

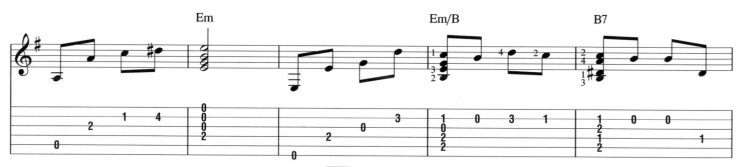

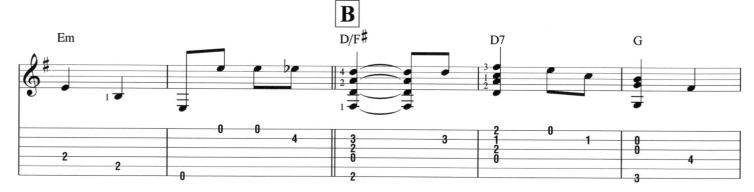

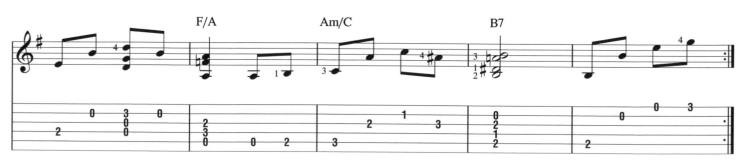

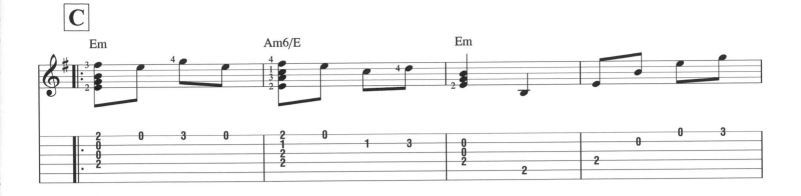

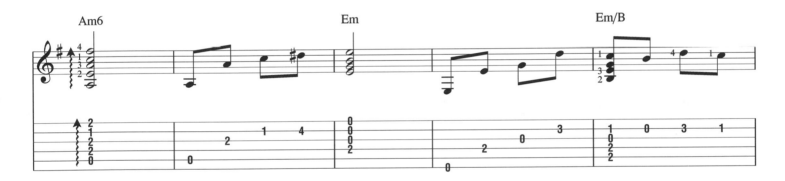

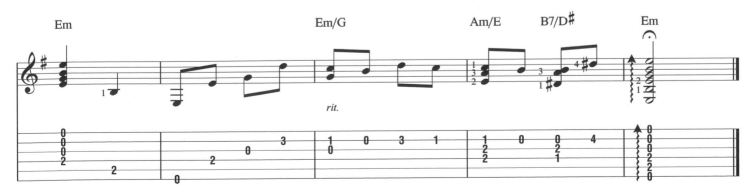

Hallelujah

Words and Music by Leonard Cohen

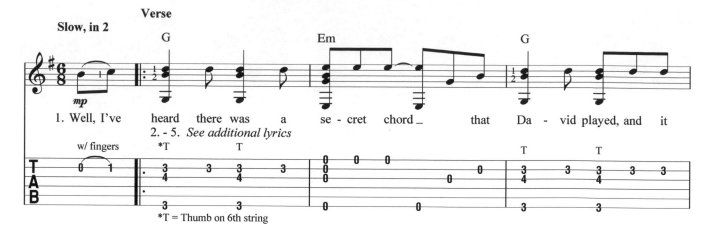

Slow, in 2

Verse

1. Well, I've heard there was a se-cret chord _ that Da - vid played, and it
2. - 5. *See additional lyrics*

w/ fingers *T = Thumb on 6th string

pleased the Lord, but you don't _ real - ly care for mu - sic,

do ya? _ Well, it goes like this: the

fourth, the fifth, the mi - nor fall, and the ma - jor lift. The

baf - fled king com - pos - ing "Hal - le - lu - jah."

𝄋 Chorus

Hal - le - lu - jah, ha - le -

lu - jah, ha - le - lu - jah,

6th time, To Coda ⊕ | 1. - 4.

ha - le - lu -

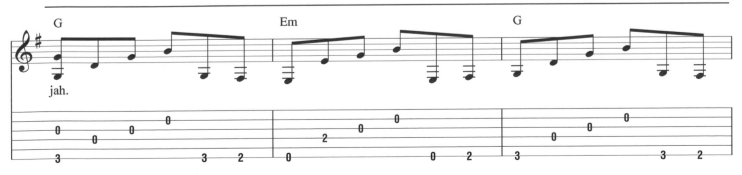

jah.

D.S. al Coda

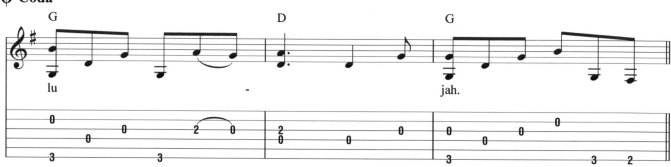

Additional Lyrics

2. Well, your faith was strong, but you needed proof.
   You saw her bathing on the roof.
   Her beauty and the moonlight overthrew ya.
   She tied you to her kitchen chair,
   And she broke your throne and she cut your hair,
   And from your lips she drew the hallelujah.

3. Well, baby, I've been here before,
   I've seen this room and I've walked this floor,
   You know, I used to live alone before I knew ya.
   And I've seen your flag on the marble arch,
   And love is not a vict'ry march,
   It's a cold and it's a broken hallelujah.

4. Well, there was a time when you let me know
   What's really going on below.
   But now you never show that to me, do ya?
   But remember when I moved in you
   And the holy dove was moving too,
   And ev'ry breath we drew was hallelujah.

5. Maybe there is a God above,
   But all I've ever learned from love
   Was how to shoot somebody who outdrew ya.
   And it's not a cry that you hear at night,
   It's not somebody who's seen the light,
   It's a cold and it's a broken hallelujah.

Happy Birthday to You

Words and Music by Mildred J. Hill and Patty S. Hill

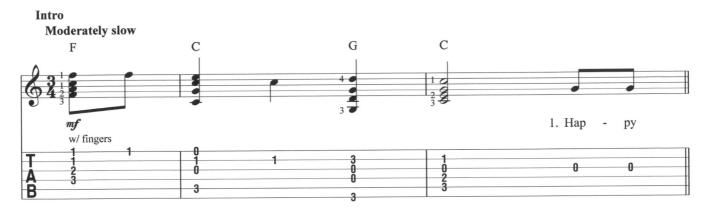

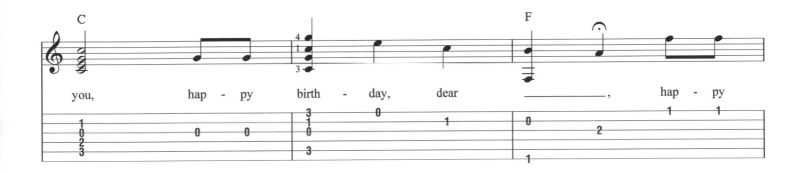

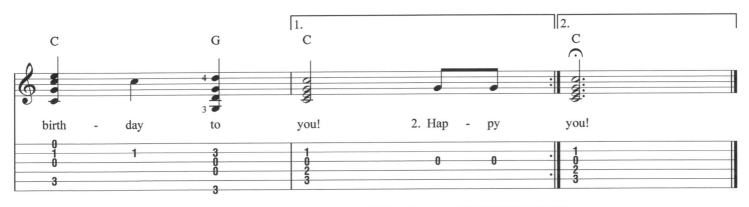

In My Life

Words and Music by John Lennon and Paul McCartney

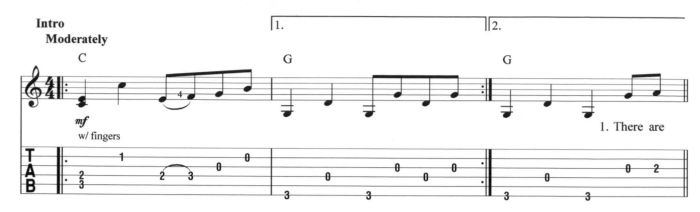

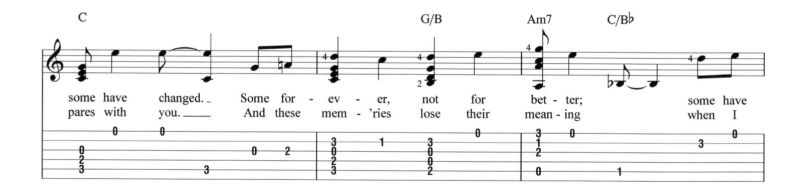

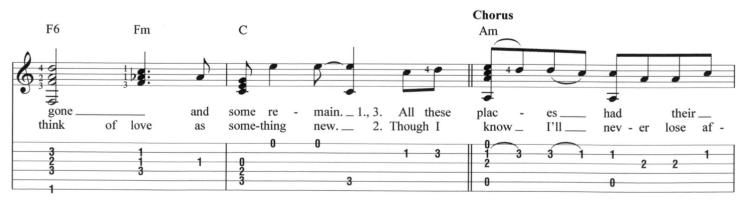

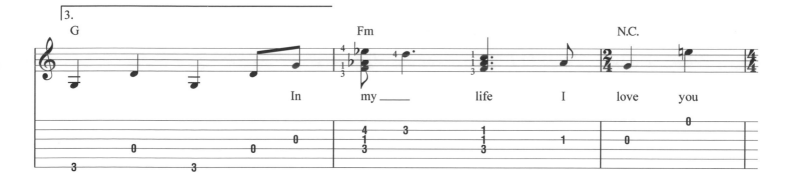

Lean on Me

Words and Music by Bill Withers

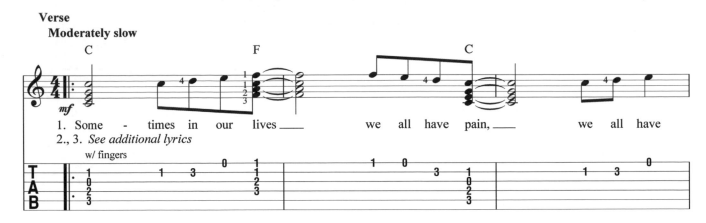

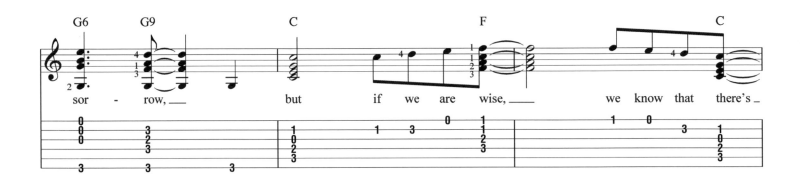

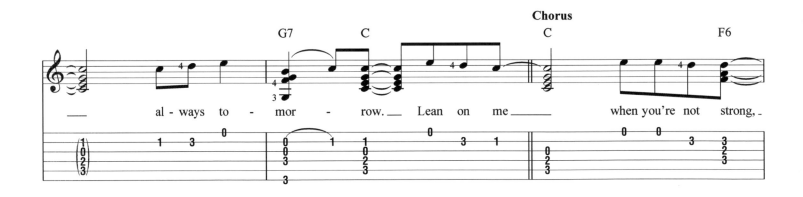

3rd time, To Coda ⊕

for   it   won't   be   long _____   till   I'm   gon - na   need _____   some - bod - y   to

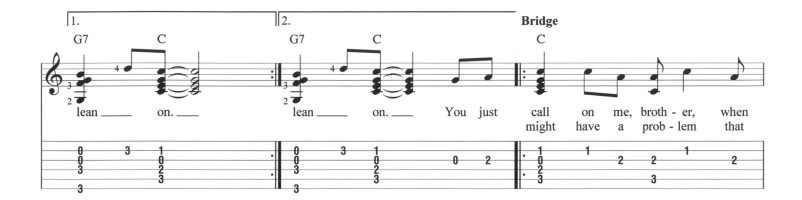

lean _____   on. _____ / lean _____   on. _____   You   just   call   on   me,   broth - er,   when
                                                                            might   have   a   prob - lem   that

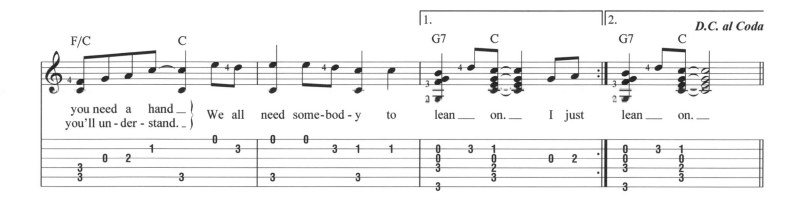

you need a   hand _ }   We   all   need   some - bod - y   to   lean _____   on. _____   I   just   lean _____   on. _____
you'll un - der - stand. _ }

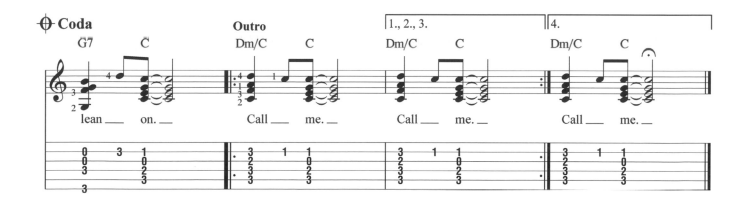

lean _____   on. _____   Call _____   me. _____   Call _____   me. _____   Call _____   me. _____

Additional Lyrics

2. Please swallow your pride if I have things you need to borrow,
   For no one can fill those of your needs that you won't let show.

3. If there is a load you have to bear that you can't carry,
   I'm right up the road. I'll share your load if you just call me.

Moon River

from the Paramount Picture BREAKFAST AT TIFFANY'S
Words by Johnny Mercer
Music by Henry Mancini

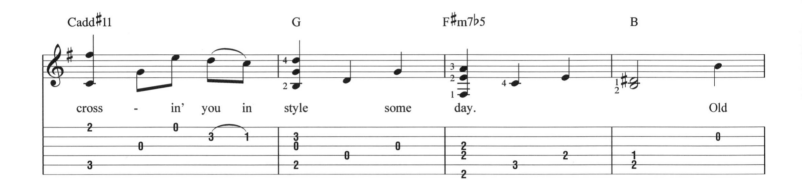

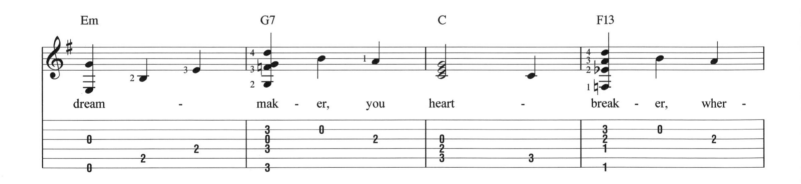

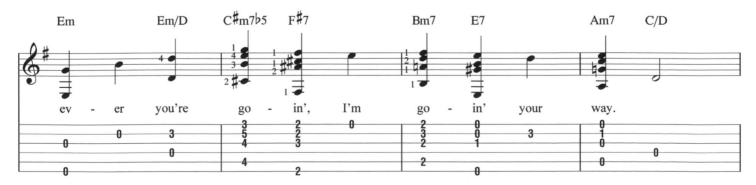

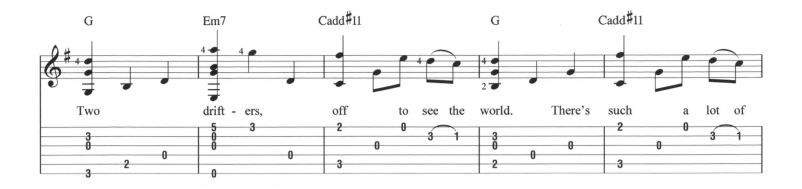

Two drift - ers, off to see the world. There's such a lot of

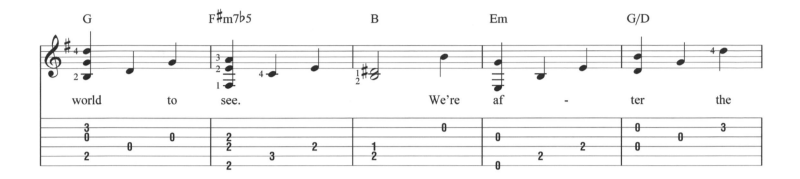

world to see. We're af - ter the

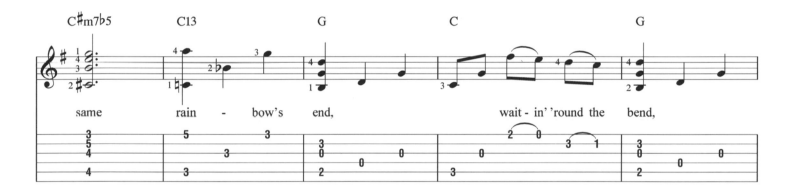

same rain - bow's end, wait - in' 'round the bend,

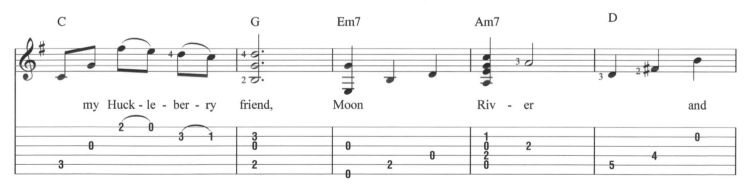

my Huck - le - ber - ry friend, Moon Riv - er and

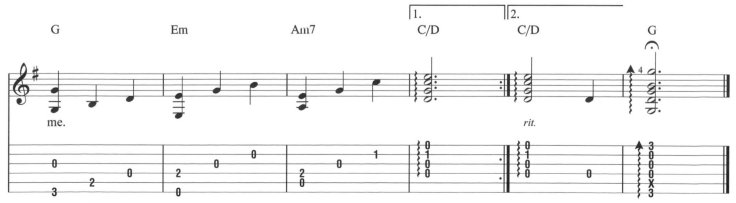

me.

rit.

No Woman No Cry

Words and Music by Vincent Ford

when we used to sit in the gov - ern - ment yard in

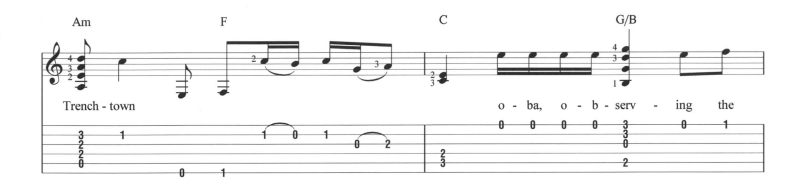

Trench - town o - ba, o - b - serv - ing the

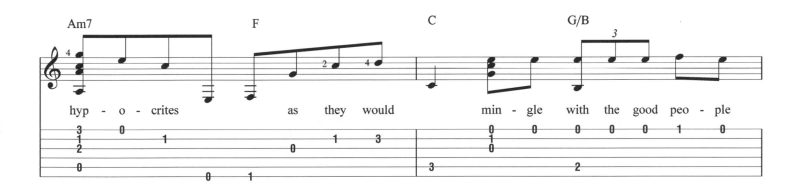

hyp - o - crites as they would min - gle with the good peo - ple

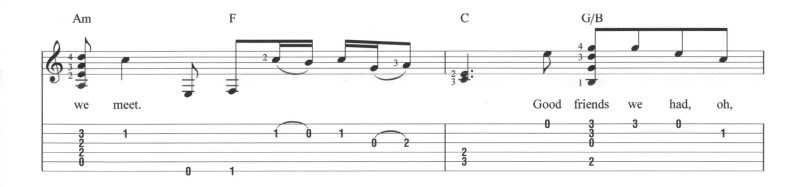

we meet. Good friends we had, oh,

good friends we've lost _____ a - long the way. __

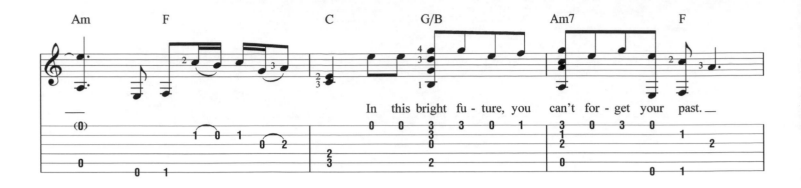

Bridge

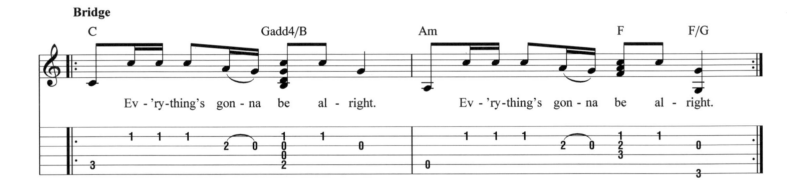

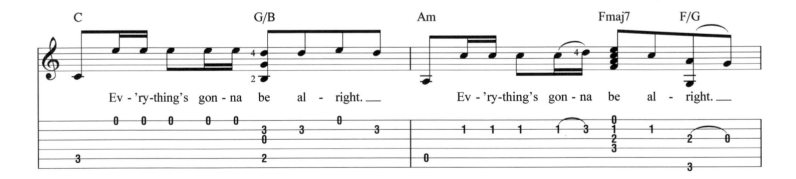

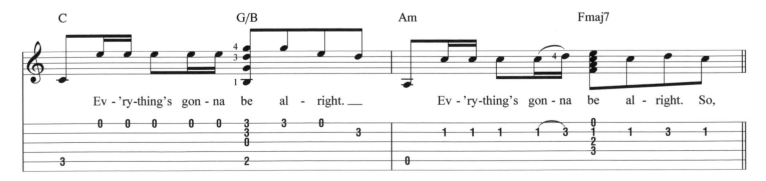

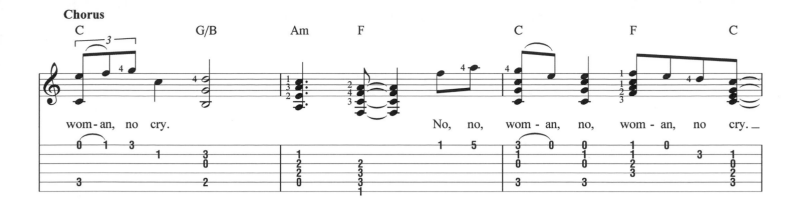

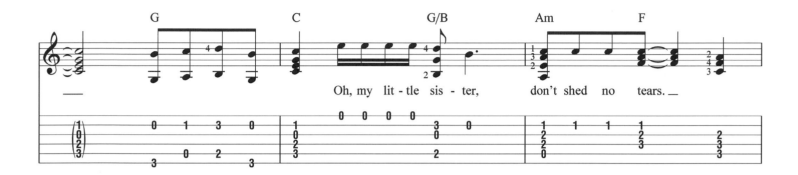

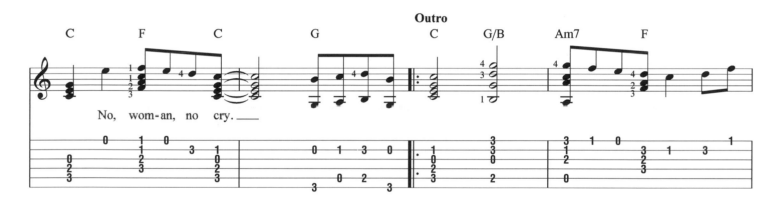

Additional Lyrics

2. Said I remember when we used to sit
   In the government yard in Trenchtown,
   And then Georgie would make a firelight
   As it was logwood burnin' through the night.
   Then we would cook corn meal porridge
   Of which I'll share with you.
   My feet is my only carriage,
   So, I've got to push on through,
   But while I'm gone, I mean...

Over the Rainbow

from THE WIZARD OF OZ

Music by Harold Arlen
Lyric by E.Y. "Yip" Harburg

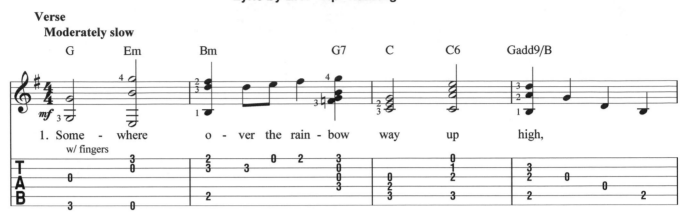

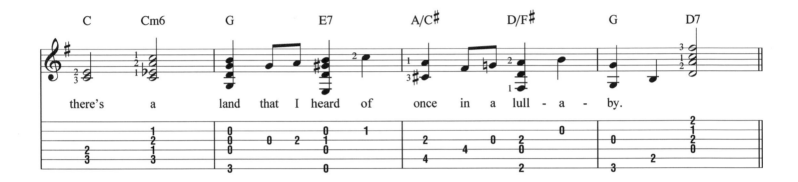

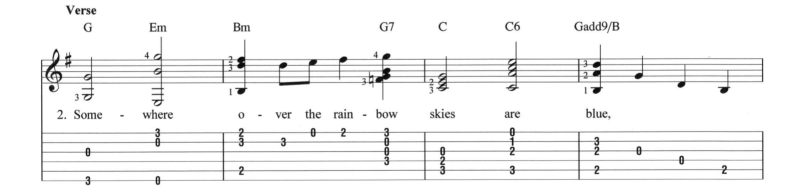

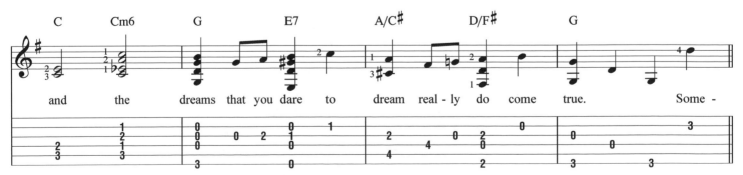

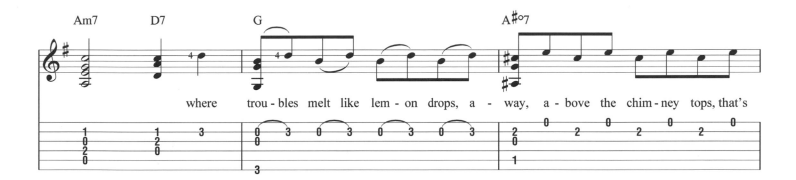

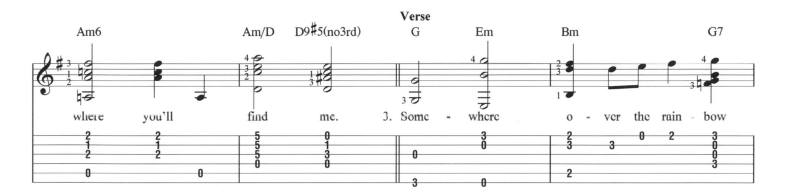

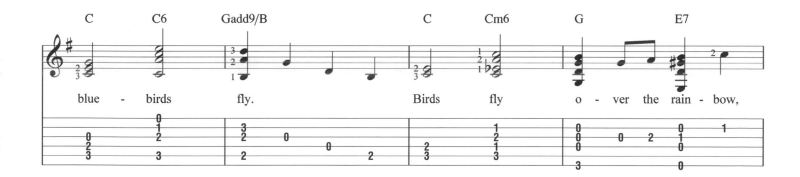

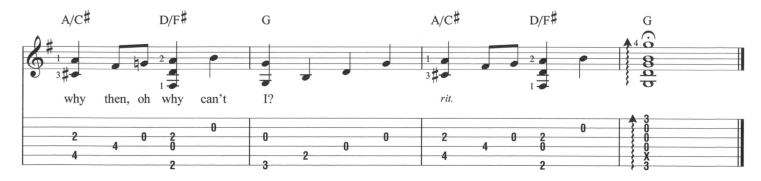

Scarborough Fair/Canticle

Arrangement and Original Counter Melody by Paul Simon and Arthur Garfunkel

Verse
Moderately

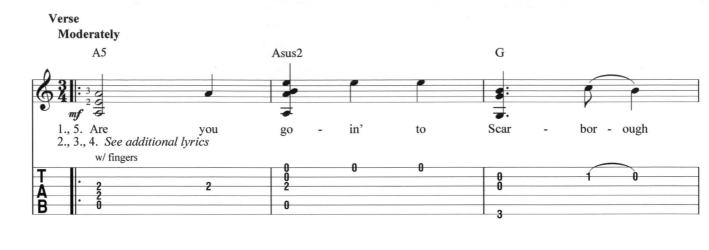

1., 5. Are you go - in' to Scar - bor - ough
2., 3., 4. *See additional lyrics*

w/ fingers

Fair? Pars - ley,

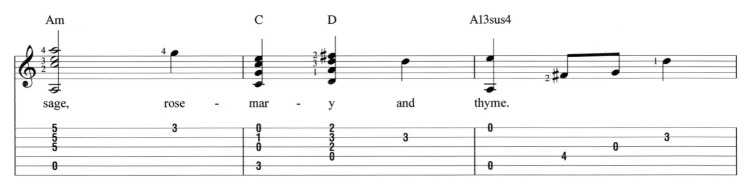

sage, rose - mar - y and thyme.

Re -

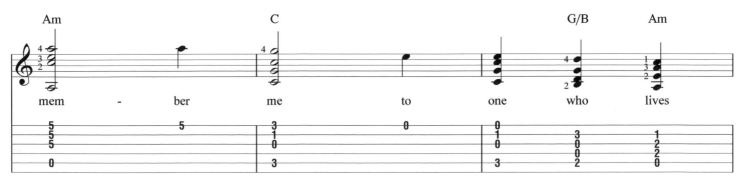

mem - ber me to one who lives

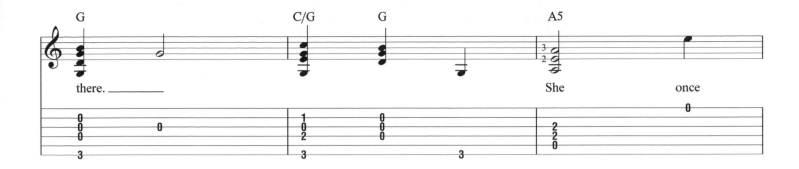

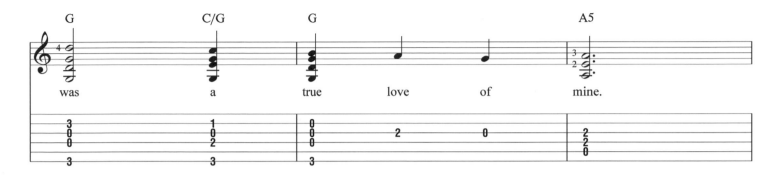

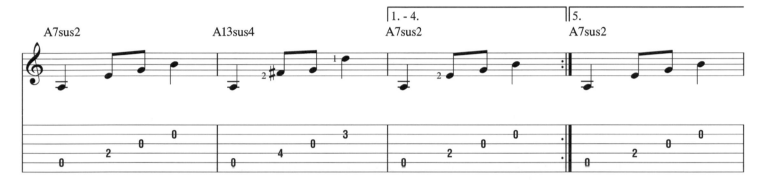

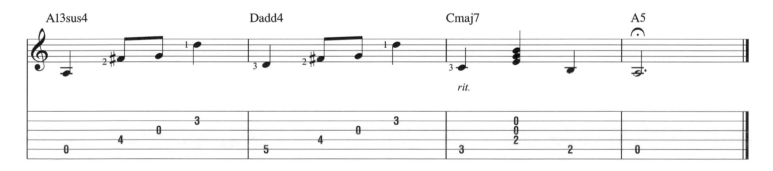

Additional Lyrics

2. Tell her to make me a cambric shirt.
   (On the side of a hill in the deep forest green.)
   Parsley, sage, rosemary and thyme.
   (Tracing of sparrow on snow-crested ground.)
   Without no seam nor needlework,
   (Blankets and bedclothes, the child of the mountain...)
   Then she'll be a true of love of mine.
   (...Sleeps unaware of the clarion call.)

3. Tell her to find me an acre of land.
   (On the side of a hill, a sprinkling of leaves...)
   Parsley, sage, rosemary and thyme.
   (...Washes the grave with so many tears.)
   Between the salt water and the sea strand,
   (A soldier cleans and polishes a gun.)
   Then she'll be a true love of mine.

4. Tell her to reap it in a sickle of leather.
   (War bellows blazing in scarlet battalions.)
   Parsley, sage, rosemary and thyme.
   (Generals order their soldiers to kill...)
   And gather it all in a bunch of heather,
   (...And to fight for a cause they've long ago forgotten.)
   Then she'll be a true love of mine.

Unchained Melody

Lyric by Hy Zaret
Music by Alex North

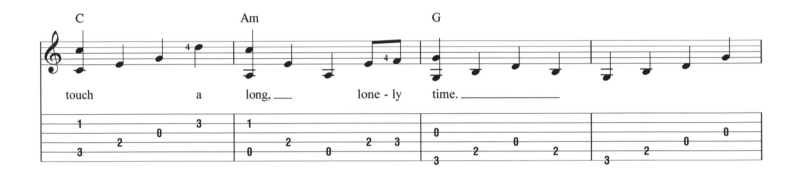

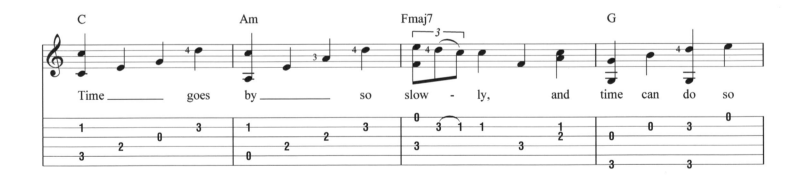

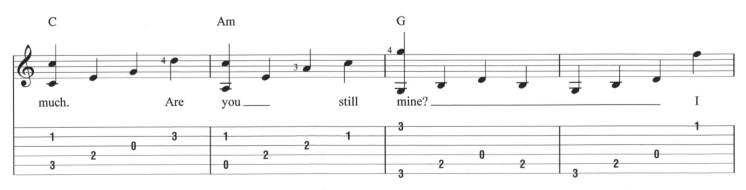

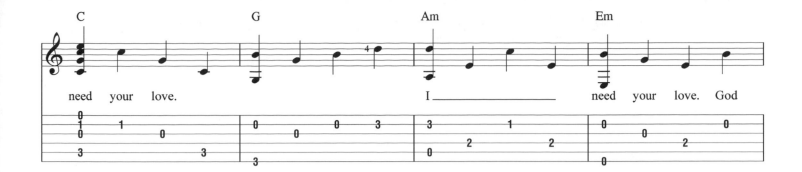

need your love.   I _____ need your love. God

To Coda ⊕

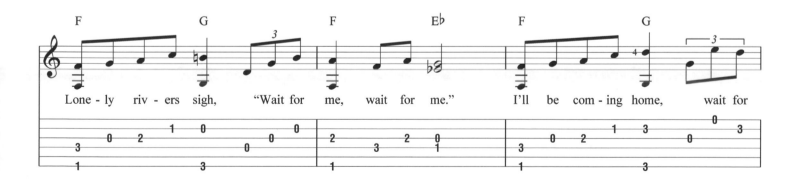

speed your love   to _____   me. _____

Bridge

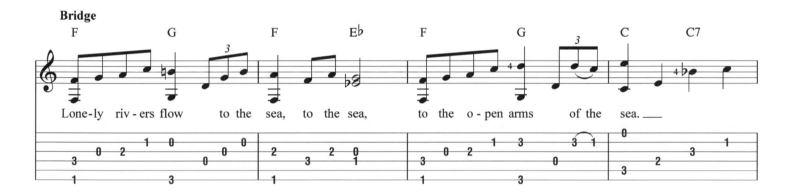

Lone-ly riv-ers flow   to the sea, to the sea,   to the o-pen arms   of the sea. ___

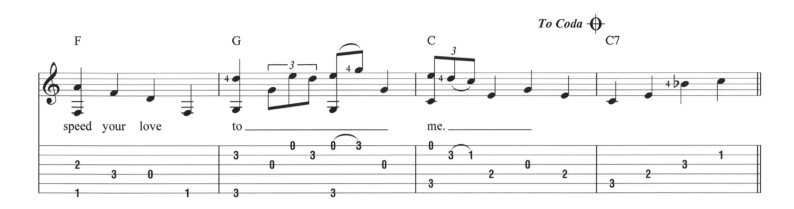

Lone-ly riv-ers sigh,   "Wait for me, wait for me."   I'll be com-ing home,   wait for

D.C. al Coda   ⊕ **Coda**

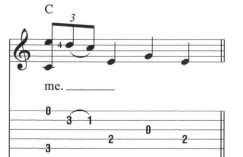

me. ___   *rit.*

What a Wonderful World

Words and Music by George David Weiss and Bob Thiele

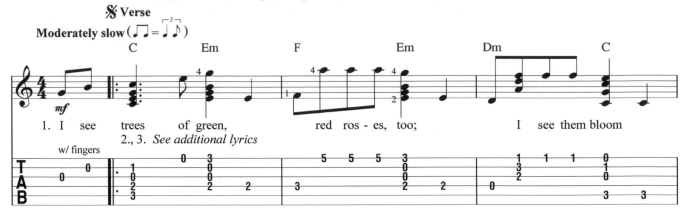

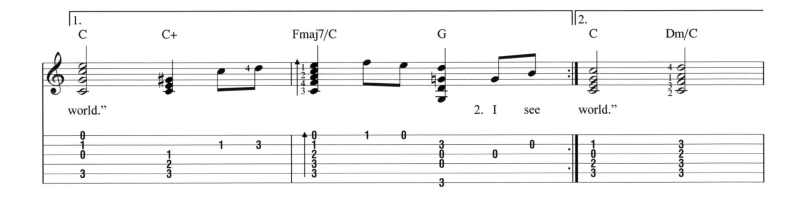

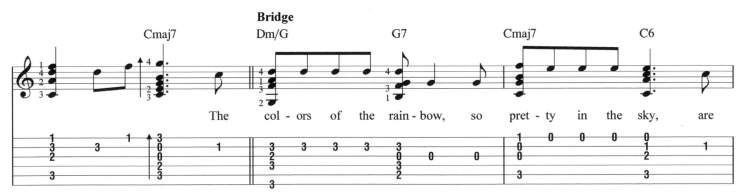

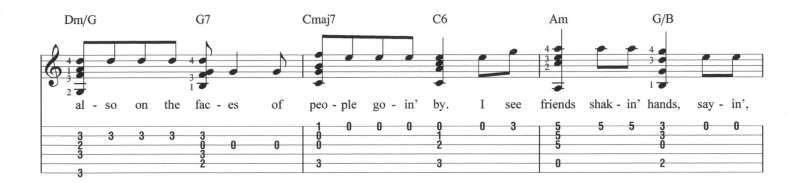

al - so on the fac - es of peo - ple go - in' by. I see friends shak - in' hands, say - in',

D.S. al Coda

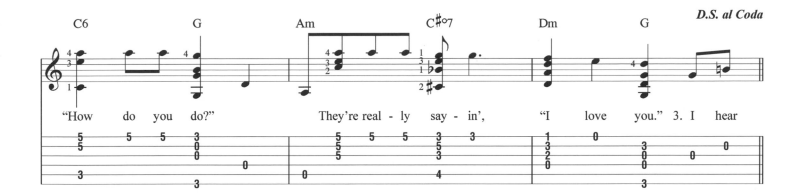

"How do you do?" They're real - ly say - in', "I love you." 3. I hear

Coda

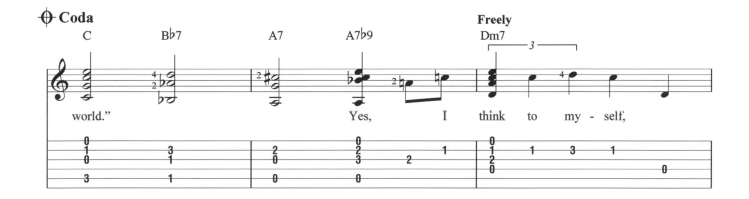

world." Yes, I think to my - self,

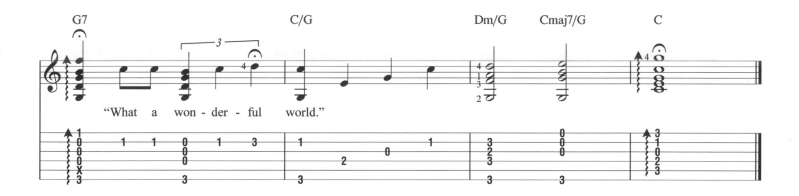

"What a won - der - ful world."

See additional lyrics

2. I see skies of blue and clouds of white,
   The bright, blessed day, the dark sacred night,
   And I think to myself, "What a wonderful world."

3. I hear babies cry, I watch them grow;
   They'll learn much more than I'll ever know,
   And I think to myself, "What a wonderful world."

FINGERPICKING GUITAR BOOKS

Hone your fingerpicking skills with these great songbooks featuring solo guitar arrangements in standard notation and tablature. The arrangements in these books are carefully written for intermediate-level guitarists. Each song combines melody and harmony in one superb guitar fingerpicking arrangement. Each book also includes an introduction to basic fingerstyle guitar.

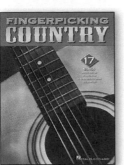

Fingerpicking Acoustic
00699614 15 songs.........................$14.99

Fingerpicking Acoustic Classics
00160211 15 songs.........................$16.99

Fingerpicking Acoustic Hits
00160202 15 songs.........................$12.99

Fingerpicking Acoustic Rock
00699764 14 songs.........................$16.99

Fingerpicking Ballads
00699717 15 songs.........................$14.99

Fingerpicking Beatles
00699049 30 songs.........................$24.99

Fingerpicking Beethoven
00702390 15 pieces.......................$10.99

Fingerpicking Blues
00701277 15 songs $10.99

Fingerpicking Broadway Favorites
00699843 15 songs.........................$9.99

Fingerpicking Broadway Hits
00699838 15 songs.........................$7.99

Fingerpicking Campfire
00275964 15 songs.........................$12.99

Fingerpicking Celtic Folk
00701148 15 songs.........................$12.99

Fingerpicking Children's Songs
00699712 15 songs.........................$9.99

Fingerpicking Christian
00701076 15 songs.........................$12.99

Fingerpicking Christmas
00699599 20 carols.......................$10.99

Fingerpicking Christmas Classics
00701695 15 songs.........................$7.99

Fingerpicking Christmas Songs
00171333 15 songs.........................$10.99

Fingerpicking Classical
00699620 15 pieces.......................$10.99

Fingerpicking Country
00699687 17 songs.........................$12.99

Fingerpicking Disney
00699711 15 songs.........................$16.99

Fingerpicking Early Jazz Standards
00276565 15 songs $12.99

Fingerpicking Duke Ellington
00699845 15 songs.........................$9.99

Fingerpicking Enya
00701161 15 songs.........................$16.99

Fingerpicking Film Score Music
00160143 15 songs.........................$12.99

Fingerpicking Gospel
00701059 15 songs.........................$9.99

Fingerpicking Hit Songs
00160195 15 songs.........................$12.99

Fingerpicking Hymns
00699688 15 hymns $12.99

Fingerpicking Irish Songs
00701965 15 songs.........................$10.99

Fingerpicking Italian Songs
00159778 15 songs.........................$12.99

Fingerpicking Jazz Favorites
00699844 15 songs.........................$12.99

Fingerpicking Jazz Standards
00699840 15 songs.........................$12.99

Fingerpicking Elton John
00237495 15 songs.........................$14.99

Fingerpicking Latin Favorites
00699842 15 songs.........................$12.99

Fingerpicking Latin Standards
00699837 15 songs.........................$17.99

Fingerpicking Andrew Lloyd Webber
00699839 14 songs.........................$16.99

Fingerpicking Love Songs
00699841 15 songs.........................$14.99

Fingerpicking Love Standards
00699836 15 songs $9.99

Fingerpicking Lullabyes
00701276 16 songs.........................$9.99

Fingerpicking Movie Music
00699919 15 songs.........................$14.99

Fingerpicking Mozart
00699794 15 pieces.......................$10.99

Fingerpicking Pop
00699615 15 songs.........................$14.99

Fingerpicking Popular Hits
00139079 14 songs.........................$12.99

Fingerpicking Praise
00699714 15 songs.........................$14.99

Fingerpicking Rock
00699716 15 songs.........................$14.99

Fingerpicking Standards
00699613 17 songs.........................$14.99

Fingerpicking Wedding
00699637 15 songs.........................$10.99

Fingerpicking Worship
00700554 15 songs.........................$14.99

Fingerpicking Neil Young – Greatest Hits
00700134 16 songs.........................$16.99

Fingerpicking Yuletide
00699654 16 songs.........................$12.99

HAL•LEONARD®

Order these and more great publications from your favorite music retailer at
halleonard.com

Prices, contents and availability subject to change without notice.

JAZZ GUITAR CHORD MELODY SOLOS

This series features chord melody arrangements in standard notation and tablature of songs for intermediate guitarists.

ALL-TIME STANDARDS

27 songs, including: All of Me • Bewitched • Come Fly with Me • A Fine Romance • Georgia on My Mind • How High the Moon • I'll Never Smile Again • I've Got You Under My Skin • It's De-Lovely • It's Only a Paper Moon • My Romance • Satin Doll • The Surrey with the Fringe on Top • Yesterdays • and more.
00699757 Solo Guitar...........................$16.99

IRVING BERLIN

27 songs, including: Alexander's Ragtime Band • Always • Blue Skies • Cheek to Cheek • Easter Parade • Happy Holiday • Heat Wave • How Deep Is the Ocean • Puttin' On the Ritz • Remember • They Say It's Wonderful • What'll I Do? • White Christmas • and more.
00700637 Solo Guitar...........................$14.99

CHRISTMAS CAROLS

26 songs, including: Auld Lang Syne • Away in a Manger • Deck the Hall • God Rest Ye Merry, Gentlemen • Good King Wenceslas • Here We Come A-Wassailing • It Came upon the Midnight Clear • Joy to the World • O Holy Night • O Little Town of Bethlehem • Silent Night • Toyland • We Three Kings of Orient Are • and more.
00701697 Solo Guitar $14.99

CHRISTMAS JAZZ

21 songs, including Auld Lang Syne • Baby, It's Cold Outside • Cool Yule • Have Yourself a Merry Little Christmas • I've Got My Love to Keep Me Warm • Mary, Did You Know? • Santa Baby • Sleigh Ride • White Christmas • Winter Wonderland • and more.
00171334 Solo Guitar $15.99

DISNEY SONGS

27 songs, including: Beauty and the Beast • Can You Feel the Love Tonight • Candle on the Water • Colors of the Wind • A Dream Is a Wish Your Heart Makes • Heigh-Ho • Some Day My Prince Will Come • Under the Sea • When You Wish upon a Star • A Whole New World (Aladdin's Theme) • Zip-A-Dee-Doo-Dah • and more.
00701902 Solo Guitar $14.99

DUKE ELLINGTON

25 songs, including: C-Jam Blues • Caravan • Do Nothin' Till You Hear from Me • Don't Get Around Much Anymore • I Got It Bad and That Ain't Good • I'm Just a Lucky So and So • In a Sentimental Mood • It Don't Mean a Thing (If It Ain't Got That Swing) • Mood Indigo • Perdido • Prelude to a Kiss • Satin Doll • and more.
00700636 Solo Guitar $14.99

FAVORITE STANDARDS

27 songs, including: All the Way • Autumn in New York • Blue Skies • Cheek to Cheek • Don't Get Around Much Anymore • How Deep Is the Ocean • I'll Be Seeing You • Isn't It Romantic? • It Could Happen to You • The Lady Is a Tramp • Moon River • Speak Low • Take the "A" Train • Willow Weep for Me • Witchcraft • and more.
00699756 Solo Guitar...........................$17.99

JAZZ BALLADS

27 songs, including: Body and Soul • Darn That Dream • Easy to Love (You'd Be So Easy to Love) • Here's That Rainy Day • In a Sentimental Mood • Misty • My Foolish Heart • My Funny Valentine • The Nearness of You • Stella by Starlight • Time After Time • The Way You Look Tonight • When Sunny Gets Blue • and more.
00699755 Solo Guitar...........................$16.99

LATIN STANDARDS

27 Latin favorites, including: Água De Beber (Water to Drink) • Desafinado • The Girl from Ipanema • How Insensitive (Insensatez) • Little Boat • Meditation • One Note Samba (Samba De Uma Nota So) • Poinciana • Quiet Nights of Quiet Stars • Samba De Orfeu • So Nice (Summer Samba) • Wave • and more.
00699754 Solo Guitar...........................$16.99

Order online at **halleonard.com**

AUTHENTIC CHORDS • ORIGINAL KEYS • COMPLETE SONGS

The *Strum It* series lets players strum the chords and sing along with their favorite hits. Each song has been selected because it can be played with regular open chords, barre chords, or other moveable chord types. Guitarists can simply play the rhythm, or play and sing along through the entire song. All songs are shown in their original keys complete with chords, strum patterns, melody and lyrics. Wherever possible, the chord voicings from the recorded versions are notated.

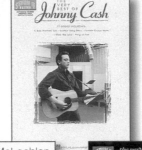

THE BEACH BOYS' GREATEST HITS
00699357......................... $12.95

THE BEATLES FAVORITES
00699249......................... $15.99

VERY BEST OF JOHNNY CASH
00699514......................... $14.99

CELTIC GUITAR SONGBOOK
00699265......................... $12.99

CHRISTMAS SONGS FOR GUITAR
00699247......................... $10.95

CHRISTMAS SONGS WITH 3 CHORDS
00699487......................... $9.99

VERY BEST OF ERIC CLAPTON
00699560......................... $12.95

JIM CROCE – CLASSIC HITS
00699269......................... $10.95

DISNEY FAVORITES
00699171......................... $14.99

MELISSA ETHERIDGE GREATEST HITS
00699518......................... $12.99

FAVORITE SONGS WITH 3 CHORDS
00699112......................... $10.99

FAVORITE SONGS WITH 4 CHORDS
00699270......................... $8.95

FIRESIDE SING-ALONG
00699273......................... $12.99

FOLK FAVORITES
00699517......................... $8.95

THE GUITAR STRUMMERS' ROCK SONGBOOK
00701678......................... $14.99

BEST OF WOODY GUTHRIE
00699496......................... $12.95

JOHN HIATT COLLECTION
00699398......................... $17.99

THE VERY BEST OF BOB MARLEY
00699524......................... $14.99

A MERRY CHRISTMAS SONGBOOK
00699211......................... $10.99

MORE FAVORITE SONGS WITH 3 CHORDS
00699532......................... $9.99

THE VERY BEST OF TOM PETTY
00699336......................... $15.99

BEST OF GEORGE STRAIT
00699235......................... $16.99

TAYLOR SWIFT FOR ACOUSTIC GUITAR
00109717......................... $16.99

BEST OF HANK WILLIAMS JR.
00699224......................... $16.99

Prices, contents & availability subject to change without notice.

Visit Hal Leonard online at
www.halleonard.com

0319
134